A *Life*
WORTH LOVING

Ashley Nicole Pitre

Ashley Pitre
xo.

ISBN 978-1-64299-374-5 (paperback)
ISBN 978-1-64299-375-2 (digital)

Christian Faith Publishing, Inc.
832 Park Avenue
Meadville, PA 16335
www.christianfaithpublishing.com

Printed in the United States of America

BLESSINGS

For he shall give his angels charge over thee, to keep thee in all of thy ways. (Ps. 91:11, KJV)

Lord, thank you for making it possible for me to live an abundant life.

I thank my husband for never once trying to sneak a peek of what I was writing, but just in case, I changed my tablet password. It's now 9999, in case you were wondering.

THE BEGINNING

When I found out I was sick, I knew I wanted to write my life down. I started so many times, and I hit delete just as much. I couldn't find the inspiration or figure out what I wanted to say. I was constantly thinking about the people who would read it and what I thought they would want to hear. I had this idea I could write a quirky and funny book using my life as an example, but you may have noticed life is not always funny or quirky. Don't get me wrong. I've had my moments, for sure; I'm not all doom and gloom. So here goes nothing, a little writing on an otherwise normal day in January, but this second attempt began with some inspiration from above.

I'm going to start by telling you I'm not a famous actor or musician. I'm not an artist, poet, or furthermore, even a writer. I'm certainly not someone who has changed the course of history, and I may never affect the future with an invention, a cure for a disease, or a solution to a world problem. I have a problem even following through with sorting my household garbage. You may read my choppy writing and wonder if I had a sound mind, which could be a plausible debate at this point in time. You might disapprove of what I'm saying, but in all seriousness, I wrote this book for me and if someone else, by grace, comes away with a different perspective on life after reading this, and if you read to the end, then you will know who to thank for it and it's not me.

PROLOGUE

I remember the first day I truly believed in God like it was yesterday because it was also the day I hated him. We will get into all that, but I had better start at the beginning so you'll fully understand my journey—and so I may fully understand it too.

Do not despise these small beginnings for the Lord rejoices to see the work begin. (Zech. 4:10, NIV)

Miracle Number 1

I was born premature near the end of the month of March and weighed in at a whopping two pounds and nine ounces at birth. This would be considered a small thing nowadays, with miracles being born everyday much smaller than me and surviving. However, in the eighties, the belief was I would not survive, and if I managed to do that, I would have many physical growth problems and be mentally challenged.

Miracle Number 2

My mother was able to hold me for the first time on April 18.

Miracle Number 3

I weighed five pounds and ten ounces and was able to go home on May 23. My mother could probably tell you every detail of my birth and stories from the first few years of growing up and the trouble I liked getting into. Lucky for me, I had a big sister to look out for me or with whom I can get in trouble.

Miracle Number 4

The doctors were right: I did have some physical problems. I had one leg shorter than the other, and I had a crooked spine. Why is this a miracle, you ask? As I got older, I grew out of my physical growth issues. My spine straightened out, and my legs lined up. I also didn't have any mental incapacities. In fact, I graduated high school with honors at the top of my class and received the Governor General's Academic Medal. My cousin graduated a year later and received the same award. I think it ran in the family.

You inherit your environment just as much
as your genes. (Johnny Rich, *The Human Script*)

I was born into two families. My father's side is Christian; they are a large family full of godly women and men. My mother's side is equally as large, Christian, and have a long line of preachers. In fact, my grandfather, whom I never had the pleasure of meeting, was a preacher. My Grammie first laid eyes on him when he was preaching, and she was immediately smitten. All my family and their generations were raised to have good morals and a strong faith and work ethic. Whether they followed them or not was up to them.

> One brain's blueprint may promote joy more readily than most; in another, pessimism reigns. Whether happiness infuses or eludes a person depends, in part, on the DNA he has chanced to receive. (Thomas Lewis, *A General Theory of Love*)

Miracle Number 5

You could say I was born with a brain blueprint for positivity, but you could also say it was nurtured and modeled into me by my amazing family. We didn't have a whole lot of money. My mother was a divorced single mom with no financial support from my father, but she had a gift (and still has) for turning sour lemons into lemonade. And that big family I mentioned? They were, and still are, awesome too. My Grammie, if she were still alive, would tell you she prayed for me every day, and that's why I had survived as a baby and grew up with little problems. My Nanny would most definitely tell you God gets all the glory and praise—when I was born, when I was growing up, right now, and forever. Her unwavering faith is something I wondered about when I was small, but she let me eat crackers and milk in church so I didn't ask many questions. I certainly marvel at her faith now especially at her young age of ninety-seven (miracle number 5).

My mother likes telling people the story about my not quite developed stomach. All I would eat were crackers and not the cheap kind. I wanted Sociables crackers, which at the time were more expensive than Premium Plus. She also likes telling the story of whenever she would get me home from the babysitters. I would no sooner get to the step than I would be puking over the side. I will tell you my babysitter would always save me bacon for when I arrived at their house, and it's also where I discovered raw hotdogs right out of the fridge were actually pretty good. Their neighbors also made the best molasses cookies, which were always coincidentally fresh out of the oven when I showed up. My sister would tell you my mother would make her sit at the dinner table long past when she was done because if she left before I was done eating, then I wouldn't eat another bite.

As far back as I can remember, we took trips to visit Nanny and Grampy at their farm. We would always get dressed up in a skirt or dress and most definitely pantyhose. My sister and I would have competitions on who would see Grampy's barn first. The driving felt so long as a child, and the summer was sticky and hot without air conditioning in our car. We considered ourselves lucky if we got there and the woodstove wasn't going. On our way home, we wouldn't get very far, and we would change into shorts behind hay bales in a field. However, Nanny's cooking is worth the drive any time of year.

Miracle Number 6

Somewhere in the middle of my childhood/preteen years, my mum got remarried to a man who became my dad in every traditional way my own wasn't. He helped my mum out, and today they do pretty much everything together except my mum hates shopping so my dad does it. I wish I had inherited her gene of disliking shopping! He was great to me always. I remember him when he was working in sales and delivering auto parts. I would sometimes go with him in the summer, and he would let me control the radio—a big thing when you reach a certain age. The band Train was my favorite then, and they are still to be admired. When I went off to high school, I hated packing my own lunch, so my dad would pack his own lunch for deliveries and bring me home Tim Horton's or Subway with his lunch allowance from work. As a reader, you will likely notice my memories seem to all tie into food one way or another.

Miracle Number 7

Let's go back to the part where I told you I was lucky to have a big sister to look out for me. We had a lot of fun growing up. I would torment her something awful. I would record her singing in the shower or even tie the bathroom door closed so she couldn't get out. I would listen in on all her phone conversations. I remember us trying to watch Dr. Quinn. The picture on the television would fuzz, and my sister would go outside and twist the antenna until I would let her know it was a better picture. I remember Christmas Eve for chips and dip, Easter for sugared cereal, and Thanksgiving for pumpkin pie. My adult perception and meaning of those holidays is now different, but when you were a kid, it meant family and cousins! I was a typical little sister who turned out being called the big sister. (We can get to this later. It's still a joke between us today.) I love my sister and always will no matter what! I'm blessed to have her.

Love wisdom like a sister; make insight a
beloved member of your family. (Prov. 7:4, NLT)

I need to say one thing: the way some families fight nowadays is ridiculous. Fighting over big or small things doesn't seem to matter. In fact, one side of my family is split down the middle, and there are a few rogue agents playing chicken close to the yellow line. I'm one of them. I think it's easily forgotten everyone is their own self and entitled to cope with situations differently. Acceptance and the understanding of this is ignored, and communication or even poor communication is lost over time. I don't know all the facts—and, yes, there are two sides to every story or, in this case, five—but I have always been wise enough to know family is what matters. It's bad enough most large families only see each other at weddings or funerals. I think you have all done your time, and it wasn't meant to be a life sentence. Fact: do you know what the two hardest words to say in every language are? "I'm sorry." Unfortunately, these words are not found in pride, stubbornness, or stupidity. The only word found there is *loneliness*.

A certain evening or morning, whichever way you perceive two o'clock, I remember Kraft dinner, Wii games, and a pact made between cousins that we would never be like them ever.

Miracle Number 8

An original text some years later:

> Me: Good news, our mothers said hello to each other at ******'s funeral. Progress lol.
> You: I hugged your mom in front of mine Tuesday night. Catalyst maybe.
> Me: (Thumbs up emoji and champagne emoji) I'm glad you did that. If anything happens to me, my mum will need yours, so this makes me happy.

It's pretty bad when this is considered progress from one side of the family to the other. Just for good measure, let's consider this a miracle. Number eight, I think I'm at. Hello, family reunion!

> Be kind to one another, tenderhearted, for-giving one another, as God in Christ forgave you. (Eph. 4:32, ESV)

I'm not sure about this new generation, with their fancy emojis and hashtags and cursive becoming a lost art. There is a lot to be admired with this generation, but traditions are fading out. It leaves all us oldies trying to keep up. Perhaps I just don't want to. It seems like it's leading down a path of forgetfulness on how to treat others. Kindness goes a long way; so does a smile. I don't believe a person has to be cutthroat to gain "success," but it will, in the end, get you what you deserve.

I once worked in an afterschool program, and being nice, I printed some pictures for coloring. My boss saw them and said we weren't allowed to have them. It inhibited a child's creativity, and if they wanted a picture, then they had to draw it. Now coloring is found at the click of a button or a tap on an iPod. No trouble at all staying inside the lines now. I think we are missing something here. I'm no exception. Sometimes an iPhone makes a great babysitter, and it never arrives late.

> Therefore I tell you, do not be anxious about your life, what you will eat or what you will drink, nor about your body, what you will put on. Is not life more than food, and the body more than clothing? (Matt. 6:25, ESV)

We are a consumerist society driven to want. Want for more money, more fame, more power, more sex. They want you to want the newest iPhone, name-brand clothing, and *more*. It's never ending. They want you to eat processed foods and so much of it you need to go and pay for Weight Watchers, Jenny Craig, or whatever. Society wants TV shows like *My 600-lb Life, My Strange Addiction, Hoarders, The Real Housewives* . . . If they didn't, then shows like these wouldn't be made. People feed off drama; they like it. Society likes watching people struggle, it seems, more than being successful. We live in a society that creates its own money-driven problems and then they create the money-driven solution. It's a hamster wheel. What problem actually gets solved? What would happen if everyone just looked around, liked what they saw, and were at peace with what they have? What if we all remained childlike, willing to share our "crayons" with others?

I learned the hard way about the dangers of wanting more. More doesn't always come with the contents you want inside the pretty box, so before you go buy that third car, listen to an inexpensive song titled "Millionaire" by Chris Stapleton.

I love girly movies. Sometimes I think of movies I watched when I was a kid or teenager, and I will watch them again. It's fun to get all the jokes and notice completely different things. I have watched so many movies I couldn't begin to count them all. One of my favorites is *Confessions of a Shopaholic*. You can guess the plot line pretty much by the title, but it's entertaining and funny. Long story short: a woman relies on buying new things to make herself feel better about life. She ends up in a huge amount of debt and moves back in with her parents. She holds a sale of all her things and manages to get out of debt, but along the way, her father wants to sell his RV to help her and she won't let him. She tells him the RV "completely defines you." In reply, her dad (played by John Goodman) says, "Nothing defines me except you and your mother." He puts so much more value in love, relationships, and family over possessions. I will never forget this part of the movie. In fact, many valuable lessons can be learned from it: "cost and worth are two very different things" and "trust is the most valuable commodity." You really should watch it if you haven't already.

I am going to tell you about something just as dangerous as wanting more: being cheap. It sounds funny, doesn't it? I'm not talking about being frugal and working within a budget; being cheap is different. I'm going to use myself as an example. As long as I can remember, I always wanted a long winter coat down to my knee. I wanted a really good quality one, but I was cheap. So I would buy a less expensive shorter coat, and by the next winter, I didn't like it anymore so I would buy another cheap coat. I didn't want to spend the money on an expensive coat, but in the end, I could have bought my dream winter coat ten times over with what I paid for all the cheap ones. Being cheap doesn't always put you ahead.

> Take care and be on your guard against all covetousness, for one's life does not consist in the abundance of his possessions. (Luke 12:15, ESV)

> The shoe that fits one person pinches another; there is no recipe for living that suits all cases. (Carl Jung)

When I grew up, there was this perceived notion of how things should be. This became more and more evident as I grew up that you were supposed to get good grades, meet the perfect guy, get married, and then—and only then—have sex and children. It is so easy to envy those who have done this; couples who have been together fifty plus years and still going strong. Many of my aunts and uncles have done this well and are shining examples. I wanted this, and I could envision it at any time. To me this was "perfect."

As a teen, my walls were covered with photos I liked; magazine clippings of hot actors and models—basically, photos of good-looking men beside skinny, beautiful women. After all, good looking guys were only attracted to the skinny type, right? And those guys were perfect even off the pages right? You could say my misconception of who I needed to be began here. I kept to myself a lot; I wasn't a joiner. I wasn't a leader and not really a follower. I hated playing sports, but it was okay to watch as long as I had snacks. I once went to a home game and cheered for the other team because the guys were cute. If it helps my case any, they were from a Christian school.

I would not change my teenage awkward years in any way to be a young adult in today's society. Kids are *mean*! Internet in my generation was dial-up. Now Wi-Fi is everywhere. Kids have phones and so many outlets to humiliate and tease others. Is this a learned behavior? Where did it start, and where does it end? I didn't feel the need to tease or humiliate others. I knew what it was like to be embarrassed without any help from others. If any attention was ever directed my way, even as simple as a question from the teacher, I would blush. I would blush from my chest to my head, where my hair parted. I can't say I had a fear of public speaking, but I had a hatred of it because it would leave me red and blotchy. This shyness, phobia, or rosacea, whatever it was, helped me understand what it would be like to be bullied. It doesn't stop anyone from bullying nowadays because everyone has a cell phone or access to Internet. I didn't get a cell phone until I went off to university, and when my dad gave it to me, it was one of those big black flip phones with antenna. It had no data plan or phone time, but it called 911 for *emergencies*!

Miracle Number 9

My sister became pregnant (out of wedlock), and it was a hot topic for a while, for sure. Then she became a single mom, but I was sooo happy. Oh boy, I loved and still love my nephew. He was my boy. I was "Auntie," but it came out more like "Atee." I had never given much thought to how hard it must have been for my sister at the time because I was too enamored with this tiny boy to think how she felt. She was not alone, yet she was. However, that baby was one giant miracle. He looked up to me. He is now fifteen and six feet tall. Now I look up to him.

> Do not judge by appearances, but judge
> with righteous judgment. (John 7:24, ESV)

My sister had help from my parents and other family, but it seemed like it opened her up to criticisms and other people's opinions. The point is individuals are hard enough on themselves sometimes without others weighing in (unless they are asked to). You know the age-old saying: "never judge someone else until you have walked a mile in their shoes." Sometimes support is enough. By the way, my sister makes good lemonade—her recipe, of course.

My sister calls me a princess to this day although I'm not really, but compared to when we were kids, I was pretty in purple, never wanting to get dirty, while she never worried about dirt and has probably even eaten some . . . off fresh garden veggies, of course. Who hasn't done that?

There was a point in time when my sister and I came up with the joke that I was the big sister, and she was titled "little sister". I was considered by her more mature and having my "stuff" together; thus, our nicknames for one another. Another question: does anyone actually have their stuff together? I believe certain people are just better at choosing what they show the world and what they don't.

> Rejoice, oh young man, in thy youth; and let thy heart cheer thee in the days of thy youth, and walk in the ways of thine heart, and in the sight of thine eyes: but know thou, that all these things God will bring thee into judgment. Therefore remove sorrow from thy heart, and put away evil from thy flesh: for childhood and youth are vanity. (Eccles. 11:9–10, KJV)

My mother had firsthand experience on what it was like to be a single mother. I remember her saying to make sure I got a good education before getting married so I had something to fall back on in case the marriage didn't work out. I think as a parent, you want the best for your kids, and sometimes this means making sure they don't make the same mistakes you perceive yourself as having made. Hindsight is always 20/20. So no question I was heading for a post-secondary education.

Miracle Number 10

I was accepted to university, and I was going to move in with my best friend from high school. It's so exciting to be a young adult with nothing but hope for the future and the naïveté of what life will throw your way. To me, an education and career were a pathway to the right guy, so this made me a little boy crazy, I think.

I dated a lot in university and college. I went from a high school girl who wanted to wait to have sex when married to "okay, nineteen is good." I thought I had found someone special. Unfortunately, attraction is often misrepresented as love, and when the sparks fizzle out, Mr. Right is not Mr. Right anymore. The problem with me is I have this gift/curse of seeing the good in everyone. I could romanticize any relationship I was in, and it lead me to ignore some big red flags. They may as well have been banners because I didn't notice. Until a certain day, like a light switch, I would be done, and my mind would move on, leaving my feet to catch up. I had some relationships that led to great friendships. Just because two people don't have the chemistry romantically doesn't mean you haven't added someone of value to your life. I don't live in the past or dwell on any of my shortcomings, except in writing these few paragraphs. Every point in my life has lead me to another; each a stepping stone to where I should be.

I grew up with many diverse and strong women in my life. All women were amazing in some way, beautifully flawed in others, but all equally incredible. Why is it I could always see the beauty in others but never in myself? I once watched this documentary called *Embrace*. It was all about the beauty of all women. Different body shapes, sizes, race, culture; it didn't matter. Beauty is in how you see yourself not how others do. Such a simple statement yet one of the most difficult challenges any woman/girl faces. I'm speaking from a female perspective, but I'm sure this can apply to boys as well. I always felt I had something to prove, and now I realize it wasn't to prove something to others. It was the need to prove something to myself. I felt inadequate in some way to myself. I still catch myself feeling that way sometimes. It's a hard notion to shake when you have made yourself feel that way for so long. One of my friends said to me once I had been the skinny one, and I only remember always wanting to be thinner. Not to the point of not eating, but looking back at photos now, it was crazy how distorted my self- image was.

People make millions every day/month/year on studying the effects environment plays on self-esteem. For example, a daughter always watching her mother on a diet. How about a son watching his father smoke or drink and perceiving that as cool? I often try and hide even the smallest of arguments my husband and I may have from our kids, but I often wonder if we are setting a healthy example by doing that. Is it better to show them an idealized fairytale of marriage or use the ups and downs of life as a tool to show them lives aren't always perfect, relationships aren't always perfect, there will be good and bad times, and hard work is involved? Would this take away unhealthy expectations in life? Or is it better to shelter kids from each new "unruly" generation to try and preserve the rose-colored glasses? *Try* being the operative word. Will this poorly equip them for the world they will enter? Does growing up around swearing take away its appeal, or will hearing it daily make you follow suit? I will tell you it's rare I swear, and I never grew up around it. Many people would tell you it would be shocking if they heard such things from me. However, I have known myself on the occasion of a stubbed toe, Charley horse, or a knock to the funny bone, to let something slip. Once it slipped in front of my daughter, and as slippery as it came out, so did, "Don't ever repeat that." In all honesty, swearing is the least of my worries these days. What is up with the Tide Pods? How does one equip their children with an invisible flak jacket in an ever-changing world?

> Finally, my brethren, be strong in the Lord,
> and in the power of his might. Put on the whole
> armor of God, that ye may be able to stand against
> the wiles of the devil. (Eph. 6:10–12, KJV)

We can say a child's experiences will shape them into what kind of adult they will be, but lately, they seem to be turning into easy excuses for misfortunes or for doing something wrong. A recent *Dr. Phil* show told the story of a group of teens who had unintentionally (or at least I hope so) killed a man by dropping rocks off an overpass onto moving vehicles. In trying to understand the crime, they tried to determine the kids' temperament, their experiences and behavior growing up, and whether or not they were a leader or follower. This may be important, but does it justify a crime or just help society empathize with them if they had of been misguided in some way. Does it make the person more socially acceptable?

One thing I have learned is excuses don't fix any kind of problem; it only creates more excuses and the readiness to give them. Take me for example: you could say I was cursed from both sides of my family to love food. Every family get-together involves food; not the healthy kind either. Every memory I have growing up involves some kind of food. Going to the fair as a kid, I never remember the rides or the games, just the strawberry shortcake and the smell of popcorn and greasy french fries. You could say I'm obsessed with food because of my upbringing, but you would be wrong. I have no self-control or willpower when it comes to food or sweets. I can eat long after I'm full. You see, I have always been a self-condemner. If I try to give up sugar and I eat one brownie, I would feel so bad I would eat ten more. If I ate the cake, I may as well have the chips and candy too. You know the saying "loose the battle but win the war?" Well, I will lose both. I also suffer from a very well-known condition called "emotional eating." It's the new cigarettes or alcohol and can certainly be just as dangerous. I think it's fine until your metabolism slows down.

I celebrate with food, and I eat when I'm sad or bored. Just because there's a bag of chips doesn't mean I have to eat them, but I usually do. Food is the reason why when I see grape jelly, I remember the book *The Outsiders* from ninth grade. Soda liked grape jelly on his eggs, or was it Pony? I just remember the egg and grape jelly part. Food is the reason I remember the Adam Sandler movie *Spanglish*. I remember the part where he makes a fried egg sandwich and cuts it carefully angled, so when he moves one-half, the over easy middle makes a perfectly curved line from one corner of the sandwich to the other. I have a food obsession. Maybe I was doomed from how I grew up, but in truth, every problem I have I could solve with my own self-control. If only I had more of it.

My husband wears his emotions on the outside. No matter what way he feels, you'll know it. He hides very little, and I love him for that even if I dislike him sometimes. I keep everything to myself and eat a whole pizza or pie. I keep everything in until it builds up and then *bam*! It usually comes out when some stupid little insignificant thing happens and I have built up for so long I'm not even sure why I'm mad or how to deal with each problem I shoved aside. I wouldn't remember them all anyway.

Christianity and spirituality were always present in my house growing up. Nowadays, spirituality can mean different things to different people, and lines are easily blurred. I grew up in church, with two services every Sunday and prayer before every meal, and I was baptized by the preacher at the church in which I began. It was a small country church, just like the ones that are fading into existence because new generations are just not going to them. As I got older,

I didn't like going and I had so many questions, or maybe I didn't like giving up the day before school on Monday. I can, however, tell you I have always believed in heaven and angels. I had a few family members pass away, and every breath in my being believes they are in heaven. It is so easy to believe the souls of your near and dear are sunning it up with angels in the clouds or taking a stroll on gold-paved streets, not rotting in the ground with their body left to bugs and maggots.

When my mum's mum died, my Grammie, it was such a hard time I didn't and couldn't hold back any tears. I remember at her funeral, my cousin was preaching, and I was inspired. I felt God and I felt changed, but as I started working, Sundays became just another work day. After all, if God existed, then why were so many bad things happening in the world?

For with God nothing shall be impossible.
(Luke 1:37, KJV)

For there is not a just man upon earth, that
doeth good, and sinneth not. (Eccles. 7:20, KJV)

I will honestly tell you I have broken four of the Ten Commandments. Two I didn't break but should have done a better job at upholding. What did I learn from that time in my life? That it's over with, and people (myself included) can pretty much rationalize anything. That's why it's so difficult for people to stop bad habits or addictions—it's rationalized. In the world we live in now, everything is rationalized. I'm not being a hypocrite. I will be the first to tell you I have rationalized many decisions, and all were within my control. One of my teachers said once "rules are for honest people because dishonest people will always find a way to break them."

If we confess our sins, he is faithful and just
and will forgive us of our sins and purify us from
all unrighteousness. (1 John 1:9, NIV)

23

Okay, back to miracles! I'm losing track

Miracle Number 11

The first professor I met in university had some unique advice. He said, "The world is filled with idiots. Find out who they are, and don't listen to them." Pretty unique, I thought. He wasn't one of my professors, so I never had time to draw the conclusion of whether I thought he was one of them or not.

When I left home, I didn't continue with church or even look into going to one near campus. I did, however, enroll in a religious studies course. I needed to do some sustainable research of faith on my own terms. I wasn't sure what to expect, but it was a class of very diverse people and the instructor was very intimidating. However, she is the only professor whose name I still remember today. She wasn't so bad after she weeded out a few who didn't really want to be there, let alone in university.

I liked studying people in general; maybe because I was trying to figure myself out and who I was. I had graduated high school with a close group of like-minded friends. We all lived in the same area and had similar beliefs. That university class was the first class I ever took part with students from so many different walks of life. The debates that went on in that class and the strong aggressive opinions of others I found to be so invigorating even if I was just the shy and quiet observer. My very first graded assignment, I had completely misunderstood a specific guideline required of the paper, but my paper was really solid and well-written and the research well-documented. I received an A-. She informed me if I had done the assignment correctly, then I would have gotten a solid A+. At A-, I was still walking on air. Another assignment was to pick a church in the area of a different faith and study it. I couldn't tell you anything about the service, but I remember this handsome man standing up testifying. His skin was not white like mine, and it didn't matter. However, it stunned me, and I'm not even sure why it did. Maybe it was because I had always gone to churches with all white people. It had nothing to do with the church, but the community we lived in wasn't very diverse and it wasn't a thriving metropolis where people wanted to move. I'm certainly not racist and I can love anyone no matter their color or creed, but that was a new experience for me and opened my mind almost as if I were learning a new language. I was truly blessed that day.

> For I know the plans I have for you, declares
> the Lord, plans for welfare and not for evil, to
> give you a future and hope. (Jer. 29:11, ESV)

I finished two years of my degree, and I'm not sure if I had lost interest or what but I felt I was being lead in another direction. Looking back at how confused I was, I can see myself feeling like a fraud. How could I study society's emotions and human behavior if I didn't even know who I was? I didn't want to be a fraud; someone giving advice to others when I hadn't even figured out by morals and beliefs. It's like the therapist who has a therapist. I didn't even have a clear picture on who I wanted to be. By the way, I was and am complex and an over-thinker. Anyways, I moved to a small town by the sea. It was a fresh start, and the moment I got out of the car, I felt free. My ex said to me once he knew the very moment I got out of the car, any hope of any relationship, even a long-distance one, was already shining in my taillights.

Going to a community college was the best thing I ever did for my education and to better myself. No matter what you study, they combine it with courses on business, marketing, property management, people management, and life skills. They essentially trained me to be ready for the work force. A lot of it was common sense things, but hearing it out loud really nailed it down for me. A far cry from psychology, but my interests were and are broad in many things. I ended up living and working there well after I graduated. It was hands down one of the best times in my life. One instructor in college called me a "silent hub" and told me to really think about that. That was my personal feedback after a group presentation. I have ideas on what I think it meant. Any ideas? Because I still don't truly know what he meant.

I met my three best friends in college who are still with me to this day. My first car was a Firefly four-door, also called a Geo. It had a problem with the engine and made this loud, annoying ticking noise. It would cost more to have it repaired than the car had cost, so I didn't bother. It got me from point A to B and even lost with my friends a few times. Once we ended up on a golf course path that was meant for carts. No idea how; too much talking and laughing, I bet.

Miracle Number 12

After graduating from the hotel, restaurant, and culinary management program (remember how I said every memory I ever had tied in with food?), I worked in service for quite some time. Want to know my insight? Jobs in service and hospitality are a good way to make a person humble.

> Another small lesson on being humble: I
> never felt like I did one thing well so I had to do
> a lot of things good. (Tim McGraw)

I always thought I needed a career, not just a job, but the funny thing is my favorite experiences working was when I was waitressing and working two part-time jobs—one as a waitress, and one as a cook. Maybe it's because you don't take yourself so seriously. I was always looking for stability, and an opportunity came up for a position as a sous chef at a private school. All the schools I knew had smaller kitchens and a small staff. I walked into the dining hall that was set for 360 students with an open and very large kitchen. I wasn't used to cooking for that many people nor was I quick enough. I was so intimidated, I didn't want to cook there, but I try to never burn a bridge so I went through with the interview.

The head chef and chief director at the time said they had a position opening up elsewhere in event planning and wondered if I would be interested in applying for that as well and which one I would be interested in more. Huge sigh of relief! Sometimes things do work out in your favor, and I love when the direction is so clear.

It leaves no room for second guessing. Away I went with event planning, and within two years, I had been promoted twice and was now in charge of the department. This was my "career" job and a great place to work. The people were great, and the food was delicious. I was blessed at my young age to be given this opportunity. Some working environments can be so toxic. There seems to always be that one person who complains all the time even when things should be happy. This person has the power to drag everyone else down too. Stay far away from this person because it can seep into your work life and into your personal life.

My biggest priority was always to my staff. I will happily admit I learned more from my staff likely than what I ever taught them, but to me, a happy staff meant happy customers. Seems easy enough, but if you look around at businesses, they fail in this department. Poor staff management is the reason why so many businesses fail. They don't appreciate their staff, they cut corners, they don't communicate, they don't pay fair wages, and they end up losing good productive workers, which leads to high staff turnover, which in turn loses customers. Don't get me wrong, you have to sell a darn good cup of coffee, but who is making that good coffee? So keep it good. I learned to use staff where their skills lay; I never set anyone up to fail. Make allowances for mistakes because they will happen, because of you and because of others. Try not to dwell on them; only make a fix so it won't happen in the future. I think that was my gift; the silent hub that can create a team that works well together. The silent part is important. You don't have to be a bossy boss, and people certainly don't need to be reminded daily that you are. Further, never ask someone to do anything you yourself wouldn't do.

A résumé is only as good as the paper it's written on. Degrees, courses, and diplomas help get you in the door, but it tells you nothing about a person's character or how they work with others. I have seen individuals with some of the best résumés come through the door, but in person, they had no common sense or even basic knowledge about how to treat another human being. But in the case of hiring, I think you learn just as much from a bad batch of soup as you do a good one. See? Food again!

And so Sunday became just another work day . . . again. I didn't have a problem working Sundays. God certainly wasn't a priority for me. The only time I hated working a Sunday was when it fell on Mother's Day or Father's Day. I often thought of my gay friends, and I really didn't want to go to church or be a part of something I thought would be indignant to a person's right to love whomever they want. In a way, I thought I was standing up for them by not going, but in truth, they never needed saving from being who they are. I was the one who needed saving because I still didn't know who I was.

> Everyone who loves is born of God. (1 John 4:7, NASB)

> Commit to the Lord whatever you do, and he will establish your plans. (Prov. 16:3, NIV)

Miracle Number 13

I bought my own house. I enjoyed nothing more than cleaning my own house, mowing my lawn, and taking pride in my home. I enjoyed working hard at my job and providing for myself. I was good at being alone, but I also had an awesome sister and nephew who came a lot. Some of the best times I had with my sister and the most laughs were in that house.

When I was a young teen, I would put on makeup in the mirror and talk to myself, sometimes pretending I was someone else or inventing a conversation. One time, I remember putting a colorful scarf on my head and pretending to be a cancer patient who had lost all her hair. I had a wild imagination and would make up things in my head or imagine my life or who I would be. It's so easy to imagine yourself as anyone other than who you are, like a dream sequence from a movie. I could imagine myself as a Charlie's Angel or Cinderella who gets whisked away by a handsome prince. Imagine life as a romcom. Just so we're clear: it's not.

Each one should test their own actions.
Then they can take pride in themselves alone,
without comparing themselves to someone else.
(Gal. 6:6, NIV)

As I grew into a young woman, I would describe myself as cute, never sexy. Quiet, never outspoken. Shy, never bold. Positive and full of hope. I had one person tell me I was a Bonnie lass once, and I craved a uniqueness about me that would help me stand apart. Silly me.

It was so easy to imagine a life of smooth sailing, but I always felt this pressure and needed to check boxes—self-created boxes and self-applied pressure. I could never be stagnant for long. The end result to me would be when I finally had children of my own. In many cultures, even just one of these would be considered as being successful, but no, I needed them all!

Education: Check!
Career related to my profession, not just a job:
Check!
New car: Check!
House: Check!

To do:

- A husband; someone whom I loved and is worth the fight, the commitment, and the hard work of a marriage. I didn't need someone to take care of me, but the thought of someone doing it was really nice.
- Oh, and kids. More grandbabies for my parents.

Clowning around with my kids

College graduation with my mum and dad

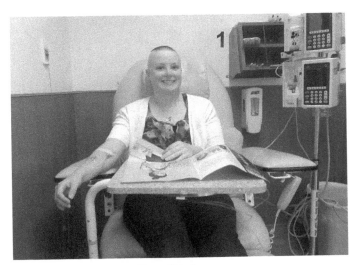

First IV chemo

My new do

My tall boy

My husband and I

Sisters

Wedding day art by the kids

Ma's Cancer Song

Give me your help Lord to live this one day,
One knot to unravel, one problem to weigh
One path to discover and choose the right turn
One worry to conquer, one lesson to learn
One moment of gladness to overcome pain
One glimpse of the sunlight, one touch of the rain
No one can see what is coming tomorrow
Nor tell if its hours will bring laughter or sorrow
So I'll turn to your love and with perfect trust say,
Give me your help Lord to live this one day.

Written by Mom when she began
cancer treatment in August 1979

Some inspiration sent to me

Miracle Number 14

I met my future husband as a blind date, set up by my friend, my coworker, and his cousin. He was quite a bit older than me (sixteen years between us), divorced, and had two children—at the time, a boy at age four and a girl at age seven. Our age difference never bothered me. I considered it normal because between my Grammie and Grampy, there was a difference of twenty years, and between my mum and dad, there were fifteen years. And I confess, I always liked a little salt and pepper ever since Mr. Sheffield from the sitcom *The Nanny*. My husband and I would both tell you it was awkward sometimes out in public because I always and still look younger than I am and he has premature grey hair, some as early as high school, and we were often mistaken as father and daughter. But now we just laugh it off, and it's a big joke. I believe I met him for a reason, and he was meant to be in my life just as much as I in his. I think we needed each other. Plus his eyes sparkled when he watched me coming down the aisle. Oh, wait, those were tears! I became a mother and a wife all in one day.

Our wedding

So let's keep track:

Education: Check!
Career: Check!
Car: Check!
House: Check!
Husband: Check!
Kids: Check!

Now I added *more* to my list:

- Sell both of our homes and buy one together. To me, this meant a fresh start, a new beginning, not just one person trying to fit into another's space or making room by cleaning out the sock drawer or half the closet. To me, we were creating our own space together.
- More kids.

Let's talk about blended families for a second. When I was growing up, I had one aunt and uncle who were both divorced from a previous marriage when they met each other, and they both had two children. They combined families and I'm sure it wasn't easy, but they sure made it look effortless. No one was step this or step that; they were a family. My aunt was called Mum and my uncle was called Dad by all their children. It didn't matter who was biological and who wasn't. In fact, I had no idea they were a blended family until much later in life. So when one of my boy friends said one time he would never date a woman with kids, I thought that was ludicrous. After all, my limited experience had only shown positive, and furthermore, what child wouldn't want two mothers or two fathers to grow up with? One would think it should be double the love and support.

Miracle Number 15

No matter how brief, my sister-in-law started calling me Mama A. *A* as in Ashley. It caught on with our kids. It was exciting to be called Mumma A. I had no expectations of replacing their biological mother, but it was a bond with the kids I was so thankful to have. My husband called the radio station on their birthdays so they would announce "Happy Birthday from Dad and Mumma A." I was never called Mumma A again. How quickly, and with such ease, the kids had decided to call me Mumma A was also how quickly their decision was taken away from them by the sweetest words a mother could say to her children: "I'm your mother. I love you, and don't ever forget that" (in their words, of course). So quickly and with such ease, the powers of suggestion made me into a stepmother. The best one ever but "step" nonetheless. This only enhanced my want for more children and to have a family of my own. I wanted a link between the two.

> Do not worry about anything, but pray and
> ask God for everything you need, always giving
> thanks. (Phil. 4:6, NCV)

Miracle Number 16

We did sell both of our homes and bought one together. That was what we did after our wedding; we moved into our new house. Don't ever ask my husband about moving. It could be a while. The moving truck got stuck on the lawn, not to mention we had to move during one of the worst rainstorms of the year. We got to our new house to find rain water leaking into what would be our daughter's bedroom. That's not all, but you get the picture. My husband looks back on that day so fondly. Oh, and it's a miracle because our marriage survived the move.

Miracle Number 17

How can you tell if a man really loves you? He goes in for a vasectomy reversal just for you!

Never once have I questioned his commitment to me. We do still disagree on whether I make a horrible nurse or he is just a horrible patient.

Miracle Number 18

I became pregnant a mere three months and two weeks later, and after a worrisome three months of waiting, we were able to announce our miracle to our two children on Christmas Day 2015. Best gift *ever*!

> Give thanks in all circumstances; for this is
> the will of God in Christ Jesus for you. (1 Thess.
> 5:18, NKJV)

January 2016, the mine where my husband worked closed. He became laid off and a little panicked about finding work, especially with a new little person on the way. About two weeks after, I had to be taken to the hospital from work, and on the way there, I had a seizure. My husband saw me seizing and bleeding from biting my tongue, and he says it was the worst sight he has ever seen combined with the most fearsome. I have since had more seizures, and he says it never gets easier, especially with someone you love, and all you wonder is if they will wake up. Apparently, my coworker said I was humming before I blacked out—my husband hates it when I hum, and in part, due to the fact I have no Auto-Tune.

Miracle Number 19

We assumed it was something tied to the baby, so I was checked over head to toe. The baby's heart beat was normal, but they put me on an antiseizure medication to protect it. If another grand mal seizure occurred, I ran the risk of pushing out my baby with my spasming muscles and convulsions. I was sent for an MRI, and it was discovered I had a tumor on the right side of my brain. It was so large it was pushing fluid out of the right side of my brain into the left. Why is this a miracle, you ask? Because it was figured the extra strain on my body from the baby was what caused me to have the seizure before it was too late. So baby saves mommy equals miracle.

Miracle Number 20

I was immediately admitted to the hospital, and three days later, I would be having brain surgery. We discussed the risks, and it was all very optimistic. The tumor was, however, fused with the part of my brain that controlled my speech and motor function on the left side of my body. I had a great neurosurgeon, and he had a way of making me feel at ease. It was easy. I didn't have another option, and it never once crossed my mind I wouldn't have a positive outcome.

The craniotomy would last roughly four hours, and I would be under anesthesia for prep and the beginning but then awake for most of the surgery itself. Lots of people shudder when I tell them about that part. Then they think I'm nuts because I tell them how amazing it was. To see what doctors can do and observe talent at its best—miracle number 20. I always end with, "Don't get me wrong, I don't want to do it again." I usually get a little laugh at that part.

Miracle Number 21

As you may already know, the brain has no feeling, and the reason for being awake is so they could effectively remove parts of the tumor while asking me questions and observing such things as facial movement, speech, or drooping muscles and they would know if they were affecting my left side functions or not. Their goal was, essentially, to remove as much of the tumor as possible without paralysis or a deficit of any kind. The parts removed were sent out for testing. They were able to remove roughly 80 percent of the tumor.

Miracle Number 22

Recovery was going well, and I showed no deficits from the surgery. I was healing fast, and the baby never flinched. Heart rate was good, and that was the day I got my first sonogram picture.

My pretty box of "more" wrapped up with a bow was stage-3 brain cancer.

When a different outlook on life gets thrust upon you, you start having flashbacks of memories in your life and the needless worry you spent on moments you shouldn't have. In my case, I started to remember moments from when I was a child—specific moments that seem so clear it's like you were in them all over again. It's like you are a child again.

I remember sitting in my work office with an older work colleague who was very much a mentor to me. I was frustrated, likely with a shoulda, coulda, woulda moment, and she said the only way you get better with that is with age. She was so right; at a certain point of clarity, you stop giving yourself a hard time about little mistakes. As I get older, I no longer buy the shoes because they look pretty, like I did in my early twenties. I try to buy shoes that are practical for the life I lead. It's only luck if they look a little fashionable too. I once stuffed Kleenex in the bottom of a pair of heels in the hopes of providing cushion to my cramping feet. Seems so silly now, I should have just taken them off, but I thought my legs looked better with them on. I no longer buy things to make myself feel better or as a boost of confidence. No amount of things will improve a person's self-worth. No amount of things can buy you comfort in your own skin or acceptance of yourself. Maybe for five minutes—the time it took you to swipe your credit card. Acceptance comes with age and through your experiences. I understand which experiences growing up left lasting impressions and which ones I were able to let go of completely. You begin to realize what mattered to you then even though it shouldn't have. You begin to focus on the wonderful moments from the past you maybe didn't appreciate, and you realize what you still have to look forward to.

My Miracles Minus One

It was made clear to me my cancer couldn't wait, and it needed treatment right away—yesterday, in fact. This meant radiation and chemotherapy at the same time as soon as possible. It couldn't wait until after our baby was born or my baby would most likely grow up without a mum. My husband and I lay awake night after night after days of speaking with doctors on our options.

> Option 1: Continue with the pregnancy, no treatment, and possibly die.
>
> Option 2: Continue with treatment and risk losing my baby or, at best, risk the baby being born with physical deformities, health problems, sickness, and a higher chance of getting leukemia.
>
> Option 3: Terminate the pregnancy. Have treatment, live, and possibly have children later.

I cried all the time. I tried to hide my face from people as if I didn't have the right to cry. My husband tried to be strong for me, being brave-faced around me, but on occasion, I would find him crying in the garage. My husband was the one who could ask the doctors questions when I couldn't stop sobbing. I could tell doctors thought option 3 was best. They never told me so, and there was evidence of babies being born while on treatment but no follow up study on how they developed beyond their hospital stay. I am reminded of a sermon our pastor preached on once: freedom from fear. He said the root that creates a fear in someone is produced by another fear: the fear of dying. Describing fear as a spirit, he explains Jesus already eradicated the fear of dying by providing everlasting life, should we choose his path.

A preacher came across a lady one time going into an elevator. He could tell you the story better, but long story short: she was bad-mouthing God and said she would rather go to hell. The preacher informed her he had seen the brochure for that place, and it didn't look that enticing.

So there I was with three options. I knew my husband's opinion. I knew my parents opinion and practically my whole families. I was willing to sacrifice myself, if I'm being honest, and my heart was leading me there. However, I had more than myself to think about. After all, I would be the one leaving. I thought about my husband, my stepchildren, and my mother. I thought about the baby inside me and selfishly thought about not being able to see them grow up. I knew one thing: I didn't want to die. I wanted to see my baby grow up. If God was leading me to a decision, I didn't feel him that day. I felt alone even in a crowded room. With option 2, I thought about a tiny helpless baby going through the effects of my poison injections, pills, and radiation. I thought about a helpless abused dog going back to the hand that feeds it and, consequently, the hand that beats it as well. I thought about a sick child whom I could love, but the possibility of them never loving themselves seemed like a life sentence not deserved.

So option 3. I had so many misconceptions of God, and I hated him. I hated my body, yet I figured I deserved this in some way or I was being taught a lesson. This baby was what I wanted and valued most—to me, my great purpose. It was the worst decision I have ever made in my life and the hardest. All other decisions made to that point were now jokes. Not because I regret it, it was the most humane thing to do and was right at the time. It was the worst because I had to make that decision at all. I couldn't see any light for the darkness all around me.

That was a hard pill to swallow, and I questioned my decision for a long time, wondering if we made the right one. It has taken me a long time to forgive myself. I remember sitting in the waiting room and looking at my husband when a mother holding a new baby was being wheeled back to her room in her bed. Her family was in the waiting room, holding balloons, and they were so excited. My husband was sad we were sitting with everyone else. I remember staring at two teenagers also waiting. The girl was pretty far along, and I judged them as teenagers who had an "oops" moment. I was so jealous oops became a baby, and our well thought out plan wasn't going to be. I was inevitably waiting for a doctor to put a very large needle through my belly into my baby's heart and inject a serum to stop the heartbeat. I hated God, yet I prayed for the doctor to hit the target on the first try. Bull's-eye. I cried, my husband cried, and

I cried more. It didn't help going home and waiting for the second part of the procedure the next morning with a lifeless little miracle still in you. I already felt empty inside. I wasn't angry I got sick; in fact, I handled it quite well. I'm just angry I lost such a miracle. My greatest fear now is coming anywhere close to losing a child again. I didn't feel whole to begin with, and for such a tiny little being to be removed, she took a huge part of me with her.

I am reminded of a nurse who helped me through the second part of the procedure. As I was leaving the hospital in a wheelchair, she came up to me and handed me a bracelet. It was one of those mood bracelets that were supposed to promote positivity. She said she had been carrying it around with her until she found someone to give it to; someone who she felt needed it. And just like that, a star was added to my dark sky.

I remember a few weeks after this horror show, my sister and I were both having a day. We were on the phone, and I was talking about how I couldn't believe I had waited so long to have children because I really had lost my opportunity to ever have a child. She said to me, "You did everything right." This meant I followed the order in which life "should" go. If I did everything right, then how did I manage to not get the one thing I desperately wanted?

I bent down one day to pick up my meowing cat, saying, "Come see Mum."

To which, my daughter said, "At least you have someone to call you mum."

It gave me pause and it stung a little, but you know what? She was absolutely correct. I had so many things to be thankful for, and my "fur babies" were one of them.

Make me know your ways, O LORD; teach
me your paths. (Pss. 25:4, NASB)

While recovering at home, I developed this horrible rash—an allergic reaction that turned out to be called a drug eruption. It could not be cured by Benadryl. I was given every single anti-allergen, mixed with steroids, every concoction, and nothing worked. Doctors came to the conclusion it was brought on by my antiseizure medication, and it needed to work its way out of my system. I was hospitalized for fear of my skin sloughing off. I was double my size and had to wear my husband's clothing in the hospital. My heart rate was 150 beats per minute, resting. If I walked by you and you knew me, you wouldn't have recognized me. My skin was like tough leather and always felt dry and itchy. During these days in the hospital, I remember being so thankful my baby was not experiencing that torture with me. There would have been no survival at all after countless medications, stress, anxiety, little sleep, and what my body was going through. My husband would be beside me when I woke up, and he would help me shower and get ready for bed before he left in the evening. It's a pretty vulnerable feeling when you are relying on someone else to take care of you. If you knew me at all, you would know how prideful I can be and how hard that was for me. I was so thankful to have a man so devoted, but I was so afraid he would see me differently. After all, we always thought it would be me pushing him in the wheelchair first.

My time in the hospital, I outlived two roommates. There was Bunny who had undergone some sort of bowel surgery. She was on a liquid diet, and she couldn't walk without farting. The noises from the other side of the curtain caused many a laugh between me and my husband. My other roomie was a woman who had trouble seeing her insulin injections and would quite often use too much. She was a chronic complainer and not a good patient. She would rant about the nurses and complain about not being able to read or see, yet she played bingo every week. When asked whether she takes the bus to bingo, she said, "No, I can't see a bus!" Yet she purchased TV for her hospital suite that had closed captions to keep the volume low. No judgment here at all, and I feel horrible for saying this, but again, a little comedic relief.

Miracle Number 23

A little ray of sunshine peeking in my room was a beautiful little girl from the next room over. I would say hello, and we would smile at each other. I received a bouquet of tulips—my favorite—from my friends, and it had been delivered to my room. That little girl wonder was sent home before I was, and when she was leaving, my husband held out my vase of flowers and told her to pick one. She misunderstood and was so excited she took the whole vase full of tulips. Even though we meant only to give her one, her smile lit up the room and that was my miracle for the day. And so we waved good bye to this beauty as she carried her vase full of tulips, ready to go home.

Miracle Number 24

When I got home from the hospital, my friends were at my house with pizza, and after two weeks of hospital food, I needed it. Special thanks go out to friends whose meat pie came in handy when in the hospital, it was chicken à la king night. In my professional opinion, a person has to work dangerously hard to create hospital food that awful.

Miracle Number 25

Another ray of sunshine: my husband bought me a golden retriever puppy. We called her Sunny for all the sunshine she would bring me. I was ready to be a mum, and this was where I could put all the love I had saved. We named her and told the kids she came named to avoid names like Fluffy, Sparkles, or _____ number 2—named after a previous pet from another time. The children lived with their mother during the school week, and Sunny gave me a place to focus my energy. She didn't notice when I looked sick or tired, and she was the one I gathered my strength for to take for a walk every day. To this day, if I don't get up and follow our routine, she will groan until I finally get out of bed.

After that trauma, I was thankful, in a way, to begin treatment. I had cut my hair pretty short in anticipation to get started. It gave me something else to focus on besides what I had lost. And after what I had been through, I considered treatment the lesser of two evils, and I was prepared to handle anything that came my way. I took chemotherapy pills and had radiation daily for thirty days straight.

They began on my birthday and ended the beginning of May. I was thankful for some heavy duty medicine to treat nausea. My next MRI showed no change, but that also meant no growth. Still, treatment after treatment, there was no change, no growth, but not smaller. My treatments were changed and still the same results. Blood work after blood work; it seemed never ending. Waiting in oncology was and is excruciating. Even if it was just a checkup, I would get anxious, and the more, I waited the worse it was. My husband makes a really good nurse by the way. He help not only me but also anyone he saw. Looking back, the mine closing and the layoff was a miracle too because he looked after me and was absolutely there when I needed him the most (miracle number 26).

> Accept the things to which fate brings you, and love the people with whom fate brings you together, but do so with all your heart. (Marcus Aurelius)

I don't believe in coincidences or even in fate, but I do believe everything happens for a reason. By far, cancer is not a miracle, but it is a strange kind of blessing that made me see the world in a whole different and new light. Beauty can suddenly be seen in many different places where I didn't notice or take the time to look before. It was overwhelmingly amazing how many cards, flowers, and gifts we received once we were home. There was endless support from our friends and neighbors and so much love and prayers from our family. I wasn't happy to be off work, but it was the "vacation" away I never, ever took. Members of the family whom I hadn't spoken to in a very long time began coming around or calling. I could say it was because I had cancer, but should I have begrudged them or just be happy they were back in my life? I chose happiness. Cancer is most definitely an ice breaker.

God is the only one who can make the valley
of trouble a door of hope. (Catherine Marshall)

I had a hard time talking to oncology patients. I didn't want to get attached. I didn't think I would be there that long. I thought I would quickly get better. I relied more on books and the Internet for information than I did conversing with other people.

I read a book shortly after I was diagnosed and going through treatment. It was called *Fight Back with Joy*. It's about a woman with cancer. She and her husband decide the way to fight this disease was to not let it win but embrace every moment with happiness in some way. They would embrace every challenge with a cheerful heart. Hospital visits they would turn into a delivery of sweets to nurses. They left appointments with a memory of smiles and not one of hurt. Never let a delivery of poor circumstances define you.

It's not the power of the curse; it's the power
you give the curse. (*Penelope*, 2007)

My husband and I met this woman in oncology, and when she found out my situation, she had to tell me hers. She was older than me, and in the nineties, she was diagnosed as having a brain tumor as well. She was a godly woman, and she told me the story of her surgery. The doctors had never seen anything so unexplainable at the time. She said when they opened up her skull, there was a flap in her brain that magically opened and showed the tumor for easy removal. She explained it was God, and miracles do happen. At the time, I didn't put much weight on her story, but it was a pleasure to see her smiling face taking the coffee cart around to all the patients.

Battling cancer is hard. I lost forty pounds, and every part of me ached. I ached when I woke up in the morning to when I went to sleep. My bones hurt. The pills that helped one symptom caused another. However, positive me was happy to eat anything I wanted and not gain a pound. There was a point when certain food would taste awful, so my days consisted around planning meals and snacks based on my cravings, if any, just to keep my weight on. On days I felt sick, I would at least make sure I ate something yummy like ice cream or yogurt—something that would taste as good going down as it would coming back up. My husband would cook because I had no ambition to eat my own. I passed time selling our mismatched furniture from two homes and using the money to shop for "grown-up" furniture that matched. As long as I kept my mind distracted, then I did okay. Treatment after treatment, I stayed positive even though my tumor never got smaller, but it hadn't gotten any bigger either. I kept waiting for something to start working. I spent so much time waiting. I quietly looked into adoption and being a foster parent, but who was I kidding? I couldn't take care of a baby or a child if there was a chance I could black out with a seizure at any time, but at least I still had hope.

I went through this stage where I cleaned out my house of clothing I didn't wear, things we didn't use, and decorations we didn't hang. It was so freeing. I threw out all my makeup, even my hair-brush. When I started losing my hair, I didn't hesitate, and I let our kids shave my head. I never minded being bald; I always wanted to try shaving my head anyway. They fought over who would shave what part. Fun can be found in such unlikely places. I bought wigs I never used. I felt more comfortable in hats or scarves so much so that today, even though I have hair, I feel naked without a hat. Thank goodness it's winter, and I have an excuse. I donated a lot and passed on many things. I wanted to honestly learn what I actually needed. Things I had been holding on to for my baby from my childhood seemed easier to give to a child who would use them. I passed on books, toys, dolls, and ornaments. It was really nice thinking those things were bringing happiness to another boy or girl and not being just stored in a trunk or closet. To sum it up: I was getting ready to die, and this for me was my way of dealing with it. I was trying to plan and control what I could. For a while, giving things away felt like Christmas for me all the time. In my darker days, I would think about my close friends and family and what I could leave them that would be meaningful. I made a scrapbook with photos and little notes to everyone. I wrote wishes for the future to our children and to my husband. I wrote a letter to my biological father. I bought my own urn, and my husband and I got our wills finished.

Even through sad times, there were always ones who picked me up. You will find some people fade away after a while, but there are those ones who will always keep you in their thoughts and prayers.

- A mother who sends you little surprise gifts
- A sister with whom to chat
- A dad who takes you shopping and out for lunch
- Parents who take you out to dinner to regain a little normalcy
- An uncle who texts you "Goodnight dear, love you" every night
- An aunt who sends you daily Scripture verses
- An aunt and uncle who whisk you and your husband away for the weekend
- An aunt who cooks and prepares lots of meals for your freezer
- An uncle who picks you up and takes you to an appointment
- Friends and family who call to check in
- Friends who take you out for the day or deliver treats and with whom you can have coffee or tea
- Friends who send cards with promising, heart-felt messages

Even if I didn't have the great friends, family, husband, and children I have, I'm never alone, and very shortly, I would realize that.

Miracle Number 26

We received an invitation from our neighbors to attend a church community day. We lived next door to the pastor, his wife, and their five children. So let me ask you this. Cute kids hand you an invitation for a family church picnic. How do you say no? You don't. You just load up the family and go. This was God playing into my weaknesses. The need to always be polite, cute smiling angel faces, the trouble I have saying no, and wanting my kids to have friends next door. The day I walked into that service, I was where I should have been all along. I loved the music; it was like seeing a concert because I didn't know any of the words. Don't ever say church is boring until after you have visited mine. That's right: mine. The music is contemporary, and the band is great. The congregation praises like no other I have ever seen. It was a come-as-you-are, family-friendly church. Everyone was so nice, and I even enjoyed the preaching. We went back the following Sunday and the one after that. You get the idea. So a little invitation got me going to church, and I also figured if I had dozens of people praying for me, then I would hold up my end. There is power in prayer. I am living proof every day when I get out of bed and my feet touch the floor and my legs are still strong enough to stand. I thank God.

I can't tell you when exactly it was I felt my heart change or my perception, but it happened. I can't tell you the exact day along my journey where my question went from "why me?" to "what's my purpose in life?" But somewhere along the way, I realized God hadn't caused this pain in my life. He was giving me the tools to survive it. Somewhere along the road, I stopped condemning myself for circumstances beyond my control. I remember praying in the MRI machine during a scan. I would thank God for each new person who entered my life and added yet another moment of happiness. I didn't care if it was stopping to pet someone's dog and having a small conversation or seeing the beauty of a day and saying hello to others as you pass. All those little *big* moments, those people, were put in my path for a reason. They were put there to remind me I was not forgotten.

Miracle Number 27

Our marriage survived the better part of a year being with each other 24/7. Sure we had our days, but most marriages don't last a year, let alone ours with all our challenges. My husband had to go back to work, and he did just that. The job came when we needed it and not a moment too soon. Turns out it was the perfect job for our circumstances and for what we were going through.

Miracle Number 28

I began to see babies as miracles again and stopped seeing my loss in their beautiful faces. I was beginning to let go. My friends were having babies, and I was truly happy for them. Light began to shine for me again even on a cloudy day.

Miracle Number 29

We went on with our lives, and I was handling treatment quite well. I very rarely did not have a smile on my face. Just because I was having a rough day did not mean others had to have one on my behalf. When asked how I was doing, I always replied "good." Because I was good, compared to many others battling wars much worse. I will never complain about having cancer. I will be truthful and answer questions, but I will never act like I'm the only person in the world battling this dreadful disease.

I was thankful every day I had some strength, but from where? I often ran into people who would say I looked amazing, but only my husband or I would notice a difference in appearance or strength day to day. But a smile (my best asset, I think), I quickly learned, had the power to inspire others, and it had the power to lift my spirit as well.

And suddenly Sundays were not just a workday anymore. I loved going to church, not to mention my parents would come every other week usually. When I missed a service, I would listen to it online, and I began to pray every morning and night. I may have started praying because I wanted healing, but it began evolving. I began praying for others and then giving thanks for all I did have in my life. I invited Jesus into my heart again, and I was all too happy to give my life and all its burdens to the Lord.

In between treatments, I would almost feel like myself again. I finished more rounds of chemo—IV chemo this time—and in between treatments and waiting for my platelets to build again, I was home. I would get visitors from my work, and it was nice because I never felt forgotten. I never imagined I would be off work so long, and it was hard for me. Soon many things changed for me, and eventually, I stopped holding on to what I couldn't control. I did jigsaw puzzles for a while and then I tried watercolor art. There were days I would fill in time with cooking and inventing recipes, but there were and are a lot of days I just want to stay in my pajamas and watch TV. Some days I needed naps, sometimes I would fight them, and other days I didn't. Depression you really have to fight off, and not with just a stick. A stick of dynamite maybe. Sometimes I would shower and just put on some fresh pajamas. I walk my dog. I visit my neighbors and have tea. I have a neighbor who will drop in some food from time to time. I always try to send something yummy back when I return her dish. It's a casserole dish that keeps on giving.

Give thanks to the Lord, for he is good; his
love endures forever. (1 Chron. 16:34, NIV)

I started looking at my neighbor surprising me with a meal when I just couldn't figure out what to cook my husband for dinner as a gift from God. Gifts always came at the right time. When I would go to the blood lab, and the only nurse who could find my vein was working. Or when I would go to the mailbox, and there was a card from someone and always on the days I needed it the most. I found myself watching church on TV or Christian movies, and I wasn't even at my Nanny's house. If you know me, this may seem surprising, but trust me, I was just as surprised. None of these were just coincidences; there were too many instances for that. It was God, and I started realizing it.

We were off to emergency one night, and my husband said he hoped so and so was working, to which I replied, no, she was too good. She was a Monday-to-Friday girl. We walked in, and she was there. Instant happiness. She had miraculously switched a shift with the person who was supposed to work that evening.

I began seeing God in everyday life—in the beautiful weather, the sunshine, and in a peaceful sleep. I had a dream once or maybe a hallucination, but it was my Grammie and she was holding a child's hands. It was so peaceful and so real; something I couldn't explain because it was a feeling and a vision at the same time. It was my child with my grandmother walking toward me. Maybe it was my mind, maybe it was my medication, but maybe it was God. Maybe someday I will know.

> Sometimes the questions are complicated,
> and the answers are simple. (Dr. Seuss)

One sunshine day, I was told by my doctor my recent scan showed more spots in my brain. They were deep in the brain and therefore inoperable. She talked about further treatment, and I did break down. I was thankful for the sunshine—an excuse to wear my sunglasses to hide my red eyes. I cried again, and after researching the drug, I stopped crying. People had lost their houses trying to pay for this drug; they put their families in debt just to try to extend their life when perhaps they would have lived that long anyway without it. I decided I didn't want to take a drug that would make me sick only to tack on another month or two. I in no way gave up, but I made a stand: no more hospitals; no more drugs and treatments (well, except for the eleven I take daily for seizures). I would live my life and enjoy the time I had left. My daughter asked if it was terminal one day. I said yes, it was, but whether it was today, tomorrow, or years from now when I would die, I didn't know. But I told her I wouldn't give up easily. When I told my beautiful neighbor what I had decided, she simply said, "Well, all this means is maybe you were relying on doctors too much and not enough on God." Yes, this statement could be very right, certainly something I would ponder for the next while, and yes I could still die tomorrow, but this gave me another outlet for hope—hope that maybe I could have my miracle after all.

My Nanny ordered me a prayer shawl from Israel. It symbolizes the one Jesus was said to have worn when he prayed. Each tassel hanging is said to have been prayed over for healing. I sleep with it under my pillow every night. I have even worn it when I'm reading my Bible and when I pray. I never was one for a blankie when I was little, and I never had a soother or sucked my thumb. I did go to sleep once with my pretty new purple rain boots on, but that's because I loved purple. I imagine this is what having a comforting blankie feels like to a child is how this shawl is a comfort to this child of God.

I'm not scared to die. When it's my time, it will be my time, but I am a little scared of how it will happen, whether it will be painful, and who will be with me. I do think about my family a lot and the effects it will have on them. I just hope they know how much I love them. I hope my husband knows how much I love him. There comes a point where you have to think about telling others you love them if you don't already.

Begin to tell people you love them every opportunity you get, even if you aren't sick. There comes a point where you need to hug hard because it could be your last. Sometimes I buy a stranger's lunch anonymously and make donations to good causes. I want to have a purpose, to make a difference, even if it is to just to one person.

So now here I am, present day, and depending which way the spots in my brain grow will determine how I die. According to doctors anyway. Either they would grow in the same direction as the tumor and I would lose the function of the left side of my body and be in a wheelchair for life or however long it takes the cancer to spread, or they would grow down into my brain stem and that would be it. When I first heard this, I prayed for the brain stem—the shorter version.

I have started to make funeral plans and letting my husband know what I want. I write things down. My memory is getting worse, especially my short-term memory. You can tell me something, and very often, I will immediately forget. I spoke with my pastor to have the service at the church. I am always making plans. It doesn't make anything easier when you open your fortune cookie after Chinese food, and it says, "Hope for the best, but prepare for the worst." I stopped opening fortune cookies after that; it's one cookie I don't care to eat anyway.

One of my biggest challenges has been letting go of the bitterness I held toward my biological father. It was only at a certain point I realized how much I was carrying around with me, and I didn't need to. By doing this, it didn't mean I loved my dad any less or I would begin skipping and holding hands with my biological father. It just meant I was taking off a weight from my shoulders I didn't feel the need to carry anymore. I started embracing everyone in my life. I chose happiness and will continue to.

> Pleasant words are as a honeycomb, sweet to the soul, and health to the bones. (Prov. 16:24, KJV)

I began truly praying for healing, and every new day I awoke, I thanked God. When I go to bed, I am thankful for a good day and even thankful for good moments in a bad one. I began singing songs from church and finding my own that had deep meaning to me. I would sing in the shower or when I was cooking and cleaning. Songs would just pop into my mind at random times, and I was thankful. I thought one morning on my way to church how I hoped the band would sing "Chainbreaker" by Zach Williams, one of my favorites, and what do you know? They did, and *boom*, there again—another "coincidence."

> Give all your worries and cares to God, for he cares for you. (1 Pet. 5:7, NLT)

I did this! I do this daily. I have given up control of my life to God. I trust in him, and I'm so thankful to Jesus (miracle number 30).

> All things are possible for the one who believes. (Mark 9:23, NCV)

It was and is all so surprising how effortless life with God can be. It's easier to praise, easier to love, easier to forgive, and easier to be thankful. I have faith—faith in myself, faith in others, and faith in God. I do still have a hard time remembering to thank him for meals; years of not doing it catching up with me. Sometimes I struggle with thoughts, but those days are getting fewer and further in between.

If I could tell you anything about myself, it would be I believe myself to be kind and treat everyone the same, whether it be the janitor at the mall or the queen of England. You could say the worst thing possible to me, and I will smile and tell you to have a nice day. I believe in killing people—killing them with kindness. I love all my family and friends. I love all animals, and it kills me when I see one up for adoption that had been abused or mistreated. I cried like a baby during the movie *A Dog's Purpose*, and if I lived alone, I would be the crazy cat lady or the crazy dog lady or the crazy cat/dog lady. My husband tries to keep me reigned in—notice the word *tries*. If I lived on a busy street in town, I would most definitely be the house with the best Halloween candy. This would be according to those who dress up anyway. Apples for those kids who just show up with their backpack—you know who you are. I think I can be funny, and I think I'm pretty easygoing. I think I have lots of love to give, and I genuinely care. I can now add Jesus is for me! He loves me, and he believes in me! I, of course, still sometimes run into doubts and questions—I am human after all—but I don't dwell on them. I have chosen what I believe, and to those who are unsure, let me tell you there is no downside. When I die, I can have everlasting life, and even if there wasn't, God has given me hope on earth. What is life truly without hope?

This is what I can tell you about cancer: it sucks. But with God, it's easier. After all, he gave me the good family and friends with whom to go through it. He put a good man to marry in my path. He gave me children to make me laugh, pets to love, and fur to clean up. Can I get an amen?

This is what I can tell you about God:

- He can bring you joy.
- Every great opportunity, every failed opportunity, every person you have ever met whether it was a good or bad experience, if you came away stronger because of it, that was God.
- God will help you weather any storm, and it too shall pass.
- A life can be saved in more ways than one with God.
- God can transform you.
- God can renew your mind.
- God is the reason I have never lost my smile.

But the fruit of the spirit is love, joy, peace, forbearance, kindness, goodness, faithfulness, gentleness and self-control. (Gal. 5:22–23a, NIV)

Miracle Number 30

God has given me peace—peace that long after I'm gone, he will continue to care for everyone I love. He has given me happiness that if I pass on, I will get to meet my baby. He has given me hope for a miracle. He has given me the strength to carry on. He has given me a great life to live.

God to me is love, faith, joy, hope, beauty, understanding, forgiveness, grace, laughter, and peace. He is a warm winter's day with a flurry of perfect snowflakes. He was the little girl at the hospital who smiled so brightly. God is the nurse who could always find my vein. He is a kind neighbor, good family, and a great friend. God is my mail lady who brings my parcels to my door. He is the spring in my step. He is life and all creation.

While we were talking about the weather, my mother-in-law said to me, "You can't stop a force of nature," and that's what God is. He will always come looking for you, just like the one lamb that wandered off from the ninety-nine.

> For we live by faith, not by sight. (2 Cor. 5:7, NIV)

Even if I don't get my miracle in the form I hope, God has given me miracles one through thirty and hundreds more blessings if I really thought about it. He was in my life before I even asked him to be, and I'm glad. I'm thankful.

Life is a miracle. Each step we take leads us to ourselves and shows us who we are. Do you know who and what you are? Do I know who and what I am? Or is God the only one who truly knows us and what we need? Are the steps we take in life leading us somewhere, or are we just circling the sacred place where we should be? I'm comforted in knowing we will all end up at the same point at one time or another, no matter what path we have chosen. It doesn't matter how much money we have or what job, whether we are male or female, or if we wear the right clothes. It's not going to matter if you were popular or the class clown. We are all truly loved, and we will all end up exactly where we should be on judgment day.

You may notice in giving speeches, the last person to speak is always introduced using words like "last but not least" or "we saved the best for last." Just like in the Bible, in John 2:9–11, when Jesus turned water into wine, and that wine—the best wine—was served last. I believe for me, the best is yet to come.

Thank goodness for his amazing grace that saved a wretch like me.

February 13, 2018

To my husband,

If you are reading this and I am gone, I hope you know I am truly in a better place with our baby, and we will be here waiting for when it's your time. I hope you know I love you, and I wish nothing but the best for you. Wherever you go and whatever you do, I hope you will be happy. I hope you have a good life with the kids and enjoy watching them grow and evolve. I hope you get grandchildren to spoil.

Give love to our kids and fur babies daily from me. I hope they don't drive you too crazy. I hope you know you have gained another mother and father and stay close with them. After all, you are their son now too. When you married me, you gained a whole family, a nephew to look out for, and a whole lot of friends.

The day I met you was one of my happiest, and so was the day we married. It's been fun being on our journey together, no matter what we have been through. I can't imagine having done any of it without you. Thank you, babe.

Please don't forget who you are, and try to always see yourself through my eyes. Don't ever forget about the beauty in the world. Your kids are two of them.

Always remember happiness can be found in tragedy. I think we proved that over and over.

Oh, and if you meet a lady friend, you have my blessing. After all, you deserve your *On Golden Pond*.

Until death do we part.

Love isn't in the falling. It's in the staying there.

All my love,
Ashley Pitre

ABOUT THE AUTHOR

I am a proud Canadian living in New Brunswick with my husband, two children, and three fur children.

Born in New Brunswick in 1987, I grew up with lots of family and friends during hot summers and cold winters. It's snowing a blizzard out right now, and we are expecting forty centimeters.

Yikes, I don't know what else to write. Seriously.

CPSIA information can be obtained
at www.ICGtesting.com
Printed in the USA
LVHW03s0706230818
587699LV00003B/3/P